Humpback Whales

Victoria Blakemore

Copyright info/picture credits

Cover, Maui Topical Images/Shutterstock; Page 3, prochym/AdobeStock; Page 5, wildestanimal/AdobeStock; Page 7, leesommers1/Pixabay; Page 9, Free-Photos/Pixabay; Pages 10 -11, mur162/AdobeStock; Page 13, Nancy/AdobeStock; Page 15, DaiMar/AdobeStock; Page 17, DaiMar/AdobeStock; Page 19, skeeze/Pixabay; Page 21, Tomas Kotouc/Shutterstock; Page 23; davidarich/Pixabay; Page 25, Denham/AdobeStock; Page 27, gudkovandrey/AdobeStock; Page 29, 2204574/Pixabay; Page 31, Maui Topical Images/Shutterstock; Page 33, wildestanimal/Shutterstock

Table of Contents

What Are Humpback Whales?

Humpback whales are large marine mammals. They are baleen whales, which means that they do not have teeth.

They get their name from the shape that they make with their back before they make a deep dive.

Humpback whales are black or dark gray. They have a white underside with black patches.

Size

Humpback whales often range in size from about forty-eight to sixty-two feet in length. This is longer than a school bus!

When fully grown, humpback whales can weigh up to fifty tons. That is up to 100,000 pounds.

Female humpback whales

are usually larger than males.

Physical Characteristics

Humpback whales have a **unique** pattern of black and white on their tail fluke. No two are the same. Researchers use this to help them tell whales apart.

The pectoral fins, which are located on the side of the whale, are long and bumpy.

They have large bumps on their

head. These bumps are called

tubercles. They may help the

whales **detect** motion. **7**

Habitat

Humpback whales are found in all four oceans. They spend the summer in colder waters and travel to warmer waters in the winter.

They are able to dive deep, but are often seen close to the surface, where they feed.

Range

Humpback whales can be found around all of the seven continents.

They are often seen around Iceland, Canada, Japan, Korea, and the United States.

Diet

Baleen whales are **omnivores**.

They eat both meat and plants.

Their diet is made up of krill,
anchovies, sardines, cod,
mackerel, and other small fish.
They are filter feeders. They
take large gulps of water and
prey, then strain out the water.

Humpback whales have long

fringes called baleen plates.

These help them to filter out the

water when they are eating.

Many humpback whales have been **observed** creating bubble nets to help catch prey. They dive under their prey, then swim up in a circle around it.

As they are swimming up, they release air from their blowholes. The bubbles trap the fish so the whales can catch them.

Groups of humpback whales often feed near the surface of the water together.

Communication

Humpback whales are known for their songs that can be heard from twenty miles away. Their songs are made up of deep moans, howls, and cries.

Mothers and calves also use much quieter sounds. This helps them to find each other without **attracting** predators.

They also slap their tail flukes

and pectoral fins on the surface

of the water. This is thought to

be a form of communication.

Movement

Humpback whales are very slow swimmers. They can only swim at speeds of up to five miles per hour. Most of the time, they are even slower.

They use their powerful tail flukes to **propel** them through the water. Their pectoral fins help them to steer.

Humpback whales can leap out of the water. This is called breaching. Researchers think it may help the whales to clean pests off of their skin.

Humpback Whale Calves

Humpback whales usually have one baby, or calf. When calves are first born, they are between ten and fifteen feet long.

Mothers feed their calves a special milk for about a year. The milk is full of fat. It helps the calves to stay healthy and develop their **blubber**.

When their calves are first born, mothers lift them to the surface to breathe. Mothers and calves stay close together. They often touch fins as they swim.

Humpback Whale Life

Some humpback whales can be **solitary**. They spend most of their time alone. Others travel in small groups that are called pods.

Humpback whales have been known to be **altruistic**. They have been seen protecting other animals from predators.

Humpback whales have two blowholes. They use them to release and take in air when they breathe.

Migration

Most humpback whales **migrate** each year. They travel to warmer places like the coast of Hawaii to meet with other humpback whales.

When humpback whales are migrating, they don't hunt often. They live off of stored fat until they reach their **destination**.

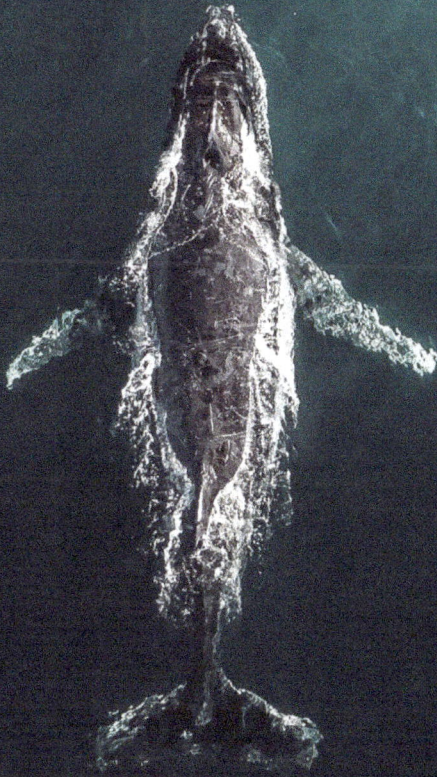

Some humpback whales

have been known to migrate

over 5,000 miles.

Population

For many years, all humpback whales were **endangered**. Their populations have been growing. Now, they are only **endangered** in a few areas.

There are believed to be over 80,000 humpback whales left in the wild.

It is not known exactly how long

humpback whales live. They are

thought to live over fifty years.

Humpback Whales in Danger

Humpback whales were once hunted for their meat, oil, and baleen.

Now, there are bans on hunting humpback whales. The threats they face include pollution, being hit by ships, drilling for oil in the ocean, and fishing nets.

Fishing nets are very dangerous for whales. They can get tangled up and weighed down. This can keep them from getting to the surface to breathe.

Helping Humpback Whales

Many groups are working to help humpback whales and other ocean animals. Some focus on preventing pollution and oil drilling.

Hunting for whales has been banned in many countries. This helps to protect whales like humpbacks.

Many fishermen use special gear that doesn't catch whales. There are also people that help to free whales that get tangled up in fishing nets.

Some groups focus on research and education. They want to learn more about humpback whales. They also want to teach people about them.

Glossary

Altruistic: helping others without thought of yourself

Attracting: causing to come near

Blubber: fat

Destination: the place you are going

Detect: to discover or notice

Endangered: at risk of becoming extinct

Migrate: to travel from one place to another

Observed: seen or noticed

Omnivore: an animal eats both meat and plants

Propel: to cause to move forward

Solitary: living alone

Tubercles: the large bumps found on the head of a humpback whales

Unique: different, special

About the Author

Victoria Blakemore is a first grade

teacher in Southwest Florida with a

passion for reading.

You can visit her at

www.elementaryexplorers.com

Also in This Series

Gray Wolves	Sloths	Flamingos	Camels	Koalas	Honey Bees	Pandas
Pangolins	White-Tailed Deer	Orcas	Giraffes	Corn	Meerkats	Echidnas
Walruses	Raccoons	Bald Eagles	Apples	Arctic Foxes	Red Pandas	Cassowaries
Tigers	Ladybugs	Moose	Beluga Whales	Leopards	Elephants	Jellyfish
Binturongs	Lions	Dolphins	Reindeer	Hammerhead Sharks	Hippos	Pumpkins
Peafowl	Chameleons	Florida Panthers	Aye-Ayes	Black Bears	Cheetahs	Manatees
Gingerbread	Polar Bears	Hot Chocolate	Orangutans	Coyotes	Marshmallows	Strawberries

Victoria Blakemore

Also in This Series

Aardvarks	Mako Sharks	Alligators	Frogs	Hedgehogs	Brown Bears	Bongos
Sea Turtles	Quokkas	Muskrats	Zebras	Red Foxes	Ring-Tailed Lemurs	Platypuses
Anteaters	Kangaroos	Rhinos	Jaguars	Wombats	Capybaras	Gorillas
Cats	Skunks	Butterflies	Dingoes	Snow Leopards	African Wild Dogs	Penguins
Whale Sharks	Wolverines	Warthogs	Caracals	Badgers	Seals	Hummingbirds
Pikas	Humpback Whales	Pumas	Lemonade	Llamas	Tulips	Ostriches
Sunflowers	Fennec Foxes	Sea Lions	Squirrels	Roses	Porcupines	Ice Cream

Victoria Blakemore